MW00335766

PILLAR OF LIGHT

JOSEPH SMITH'S FIRST VISION

A GRAPHIC NOVEL BASED ON JOSEPH SMITH'S
OWN ACCOUNTS AND FROM THOSE WHO
HEARD HIM SHARE HIS EXPERIENCE FIRSTHAND.

TEXT ADAPTATION
& COLORS
ANDREW G. KNAUPP

PENCILS, INKS,
& ART DIRECTION
SAL VELLUTO

COVER BY SAL VELLUTO AND EUGENIO MATTOZZI

FOREWORD BY
STEVEN C. HARPER

www.LatterdaySaintComics.com

ISBN 13: 978-1-4621-3974-3

Published by CFI, an imprint of Cedar Fort, Inc.
2373 W. 700 S., Springville, UT 84663
Distributed by Cedar Fort, Inc., www.cedarfort.com

Printed in the United States

10 9 8 7 6 5 4 3 2 1

Printed on acid-free paper

INTRODUCTION

200 years ago in the spring of 1820, a young farm boy named Joseph Smith Jr. walked into a grove of trees near his family home where he had been working the day before. No one else witnessed what took place there, but the world would be changed forever by what he said happened that day.

Joseph Fielding Smith, grand-nephew of Joseph Smith Jr. wrote.

"Joseph Smith's First Vision stands today as the greatest event in world history since the birth, ministry, and resurrection of Jesus Christ. After centuries of darkness, the Lord opened the heavens to reveal His word and restore His Church through His chosen prophet."

The narration found in this book incorporates elements from all the accounts given by the Prophet, as well as accounts recorded by those who heard him firsthand. Critics of the Church and Joseph Smith have claimed that the differences between the four unique accounts of the First Vision amount to contradictions and are evidence Joseph fabricated the story. We wanted to demonstrate that when you combine all the accounts, the result is a rich, consistent and synergistic narrative.

PILLAR OF LIGHT has been carefully researched and includes details not previously shown in films and art, as well as accurate historical depictions, beautiful symbolism, and creative representations. We hope it is inspiring to people of all ages and helps to build testimonies of the Prophet Joseph Smith and his divine mission.

We believe our Heavenly Father and His Son Jesus Christ have a message they want to give to the world. We are grateful to be a part of helping to deliver that message. We wanted to contribute to the celebration of the 200th Anniversary of the First Vision by using our talents to create this book and provide it for free to the world through the internet. We hope you enjoy our *visual testimony* of the Prophet Joseph Smith's First Vision. We testify that we know, by the power of the Holy Ghost, that Joseph Smith told the truth about his vision, and that by that same power, you can know as well.

Andrew Knaupp & Sal Velluto

FOREWORD

I don't usually read graphic novels. I usually read old documents. For a graphic novel to get my attention, it would have to be based on old documents. The documents would have to tell a story. The story could not be ordinary. Interesting would not be enough. There would have to be a lot at stake. Life and death wouldn't keep my attention. Eternal life and death—now that would be riveting.

The hero of the story would have to be like me, except more heroic. He would have to have a problem, a big problem, a conflict between his head and his heart. Joseph Smith's search for truth is just such a story. It captures my attention because the hero was a flawed teenager who knew that forgiveness could only come from Jesus Christ, but he couldn't figure out which version of the gospel of Jesus Christ.

One version said he was doomed. Jesus would only forgive a foreordained few, and he wasn't one of them. The other version said Jesus would save him if he would choose to be saved. The story gets even better because Joseph has to wrestle with that dilemma for a while, not knowing which choice was right. How could he know which choice was right?

I get all twisted up inside when I think of Joseph's problem. I can see that he hated the idea that he would be doomed, but it made the most sense in his head. He was a sinner, after all, and he couldn't seem to change that. I can see that in his heart, he wanted to choose Christ's forgiveness, but he tried and tried and couldn't feel forgiven. He didn't want to be

doomed, but he couldn't make a false choice. He had to be true to what he knew. He was out of options.

The preachers had made the Bible a battleground. They had waged a war of words over it. They didn't agree on what it meant. How could he know the answer? They left him hopeless. Almost. Until he read an old verse in a new way. Then all of a sudden, he realizes he could ask a higher authority. The Bible said he could ask God and receive an answer. That is a satisfying story indeed. My heart beats faster as I read it. I feel Joseph's tension rising in me until that revelation resolves it. He didn't know, but he could ask God. The Bible promised God would answer.

I might have to put the story down at this point and relax, not sure I can handle more tension, but I might not be able to stop reading. The story is just getting good. It is obvious that the first revelation is setting up something bigger. I would have to keep reading.

I won't give away the ending but trust me, it's intense. The reversals ramp up. Stakes are raised. Soon Good and Evil are vying for Joseph's soul in the woods of western New York. Everything depends on what he decides to do when The Bad Guy has closed in and all is lost. The ending is so satisfying.

I've studied this story for many years. I learned that Joseph soon had another dilemma. Young, naïve Joseph didn't know it was a dilemma until a few days later, when he shared his experience with a minister who had encouraged him. The minister rejected him, to his surprise. Joseph had no confidence in his ability to resolve his first dilemma. The answer to his prayer solved that. Jesus forgave his sins. But now that his first attempt to share his story failed, he lost confidence in his ability to tell it. He decided to keep it to himself.

Eventually, however, he had to tell it. The dilemma became severe because he wasn't a good writer. His experience was easier to explain than it was to write, but he couldn't even explain it entirely. What he saw in the woods defied all description. So how could he tell the story the world needed to know and that he lacked the power to tell? He tried to tell it over and over, doing the best he could with what he called the "prison of . . . paper, pen, and ink."

Joseph tried to get people to help him tell his story—people who had talents he lacked. He liked Orson Pratt's version a lot. He would love what Andrew and Sal have done with Pillar of Light. They used all of the old documents, just like I do. They decided to leave out the boring analysis, and they added spectacular graphics instead. Andrew and Sal's story of Joseph's First Vision is accurate. It is true to Joseph's accounts. Plus, with its stunning graphics, Pillar of Light is the best thing I have seen at describing what defies description.

Make this story yours. Find yourself in it. Take your dilemmas to God. Ask Him in faith. I don't know if you'll see God and Christ in a pillar of light, but you can know that Joseph did. It's okay if the hero of the story you're about to read is like you, except maybe just slightly more heroic. Anyone who lacks wisdom can ask of God. He knew Joseph's name, forgave his sins, and answered his questions. He'll do that for you too.

Steven C. Harper

STEVEN C. HARPER earned a PhD in early American history from Lehigh University, where he was Lawrence Henry Gipson Fellow. He taught at Brigham Young University campuses in Hawaii and Utah, and served as a volume editor of The Joseph Smith Papers and later as managing historian and a general editor of *Saints: The Story of The Church of Jesus Christ in the Latter Days.* He is also the author of dozens of articles and several books on early Latter-day Saint history including *First Vision: Memory and Mormon Origins (2019)* and *Joseph Smith's First Vision (2012).* He is currently editor of BYU Studies Quarterly and professor of Church History and Doctrine at Brigham Young University.

I DON'T BLAME ANYONE FOR NOT BELIEVING MY STORY. IF I HADN'T EXPERIENCED WHAT I HAD, **I COULD NOT HAVE BELIEVED IT MYSELF.**

PILLAR OF LIGHT
Joseph Smith's First Vision

WRITTEN FROM THE PROPHET JOSEPH SMITH'S OWN ACCOUNTS AND FROM THOSE WHO HEARD HIM TELL HIS EXPERIENCE FIRSTHAND.

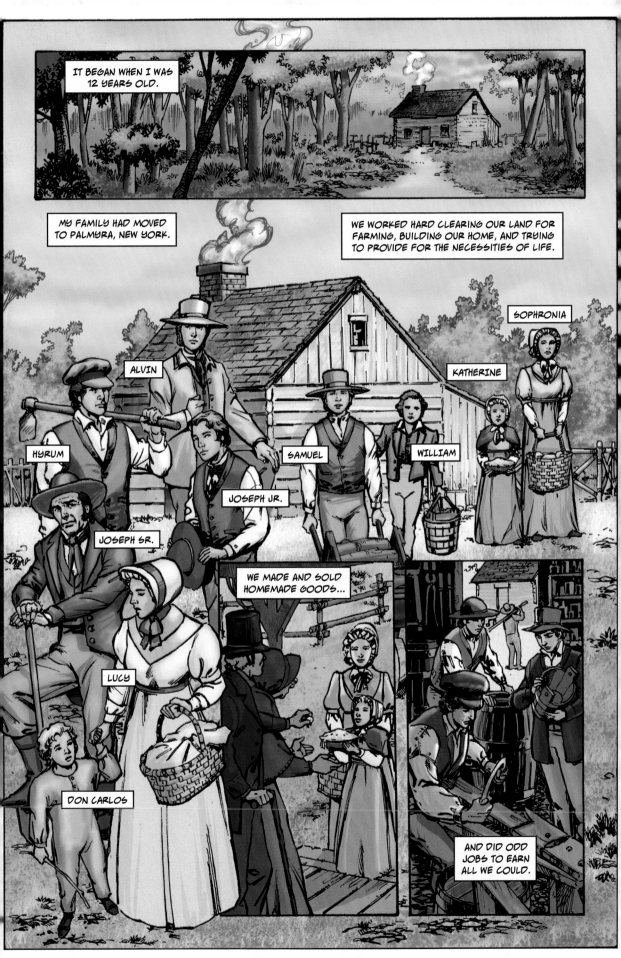

ALTHOUGH I HAD NEVER TRIED TO PRAY OUT LOUD BEFORE, I WAS DETERMINED TO DO AS JAMES DIRECTED.

I WALKED TO A GROVE OF TREES NEAR MY HOME.

IT WAS ON THE MORNING OF A BEAUTIFUL CLEAR DAY.

EARLY IN THE SPRING OF 1820.

I RETIRED TO A QUIET AREA OF THE WOODS MY FATHER AND I HAD BEEN CLEARING AND WHERE I HAD LEFT MY AX THE DAY BEFORE.

HAVING LOOKED AROUND ME AND FINDING MYSELF ALONE...

I KNELT DOWN TO OFFER UP THE DESIRES OF MY HEART TO GOD.

THICK DARKNESS
GATHERED AROUND ME

AS A POWERFUL DARK
PRESENCE ENDEAVORED TO
DESTROY ME COMPLETELY.

I SAW A PILLAR OF LIGHT, ABOVE THE BRIGHTNESS OF THE SUN, DIRECTLY OVER MY HEAD,

WHICH GRADUALLY DESCENDED TOWARDS ME.

IT NO SOONER APPEARED THAN I FOUND MYSELF DELIVERED FROM THE ENEMY WHICH HELD ME BOUND.

BY THE TIME THE LIGHT REACHED THE TREES, THE WHOLE WILDERNESS, FOR SOME DISTANCE AROUND WAS ILLUMINATED IN A MOST GLORIOUS AND BRILLIANT MANNER.

I EXPECTED TO SEE THE LEAVES AND BOUGHS OF THE TREES CONSUMED BY THE GLORIOUS FIRE...

BUT WHEN THEY WERE NOT, I WAS ENCOURAGED AND HAD HOPE THAT I MIGHT ENDURE ITS PRESENCE.

AS THE PILLAR CAME NEARER MY MIND WAS TAKEN AWAY FROM THE OBJECTS WITH WHICH I WAS SURROUNDED.

I SAW A PERSONAGE IN THE LIGHT.

AFTER A TIME A SECOND PERSONAGE CAME TO THE SIDE OF THE FIRST.

THE BRIGHTNESS AND GLORY OF THESE TWO BEINGS DEFIES ALL DESCRIPTION.

THEY EXACTLY RESEMBLED EACH OTHER IN FORM AND LIKENESS.

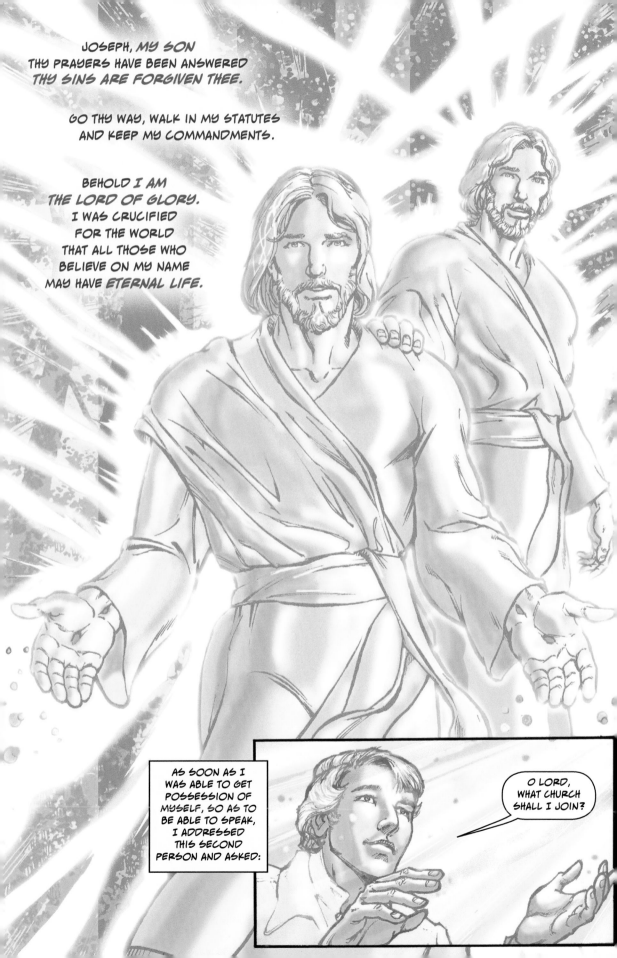

I ALSO SAW MANY ANGELS.

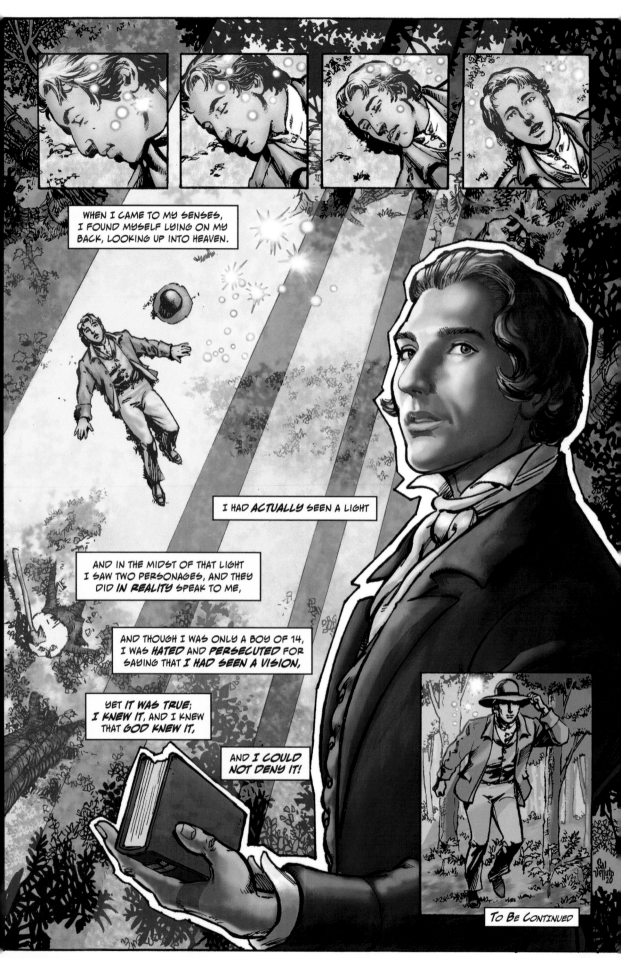

EXPLANATION OF THE SOURCE MATERIAL

PRIMARY ACCOUNTS

During his lifetime, Joseph Smith created two accounts of the First Vision intended for publication. Two additional accounts were recorded by him in his journal and by a scribe but were not published until the 1960s when they were rediscovered by church historians. Below is a brief description of each account and the more distinctive points that appear in PILLAR OF LIGHT.

1832 Account

This is the earliest account of the First Vision, and was written by Joseph himself in a small journal, but never published. Joseph mentions his concerns about his own salvation, and that he began his search at age 12. He mentions his observance of the sun, moon, stars and God's creations moving in harmony as evidence of a divine creator. He tells of being told that his sins are forgiven, and the Savior speaking of his crucifixion and atonement for all mankind. Joseph tells of feeling love for many days and that he could find no one who would believe the vision.

1835 Account

This account was recorded by Joseph's scribe Warren Parrish after Joseph told his account to Robert Matthews, a visitor to Kirtland, Ohio. This telling gives the specific details about hearing walking behind him, springing to his feet and looking for the source, and his tongue being swollen in his mouth. He also describes the pillar as fire and flame, and that it was spread all around but nothing was consumed by it. He tells how he saw one personage first, then the second after a time. This account also notes the presence of many angels separate from the personages.

1838 Account

This is the best known and longest account. It is included in the Pearl of Great Price and was the first account Joseph created for publication to the world. Joseph speaks of the confusion among all the churches, his desire to know specifically which church to join, his reading of James 1:5 and the deep feeling that it created. He describes the intensity of his conflict with and the reality of Satan using the expression "doomed to sudden destruction." He also includes the detail that many more things were revealed to him than he recorded.

1842 Account

This was Joseph's second account intended for publication. It was created in response to a request for information and intended for an audience unfamiliar with it. Joseph speaks of the personages exactly resembling each other in form and likeness. He includes the details that he was specifically commanded to "go not after" the other churches- that none was acknowledged of God as His church and kingdom and that he was promised he would receive the fullness of the gospel at some future time.

SECONDHAND ACCOUNTS

Five accounts were written by those who heard Joseph Smith speak about his vision. Some details from these accounts were used in PILLAR OF LIGHT.

Orson Pratt, 1840

Pratt mentions the importance of James 1:5 to Joseph and that reading it was like "a light shining forth in a dark place, to guide him to the path in which he should walk." He mentions that Joseph expected to see the trees catch fire when the pillar descended and that the pillar descended gradually. He mentions that after seeing that the trees were not consumed, that Joseph had hopes that he might endure it.

Orson Hyde, 1842

Originally published in German, Orson Hyde mentions that during the battle with Satan, Joseph's mind was assaulted with doubts and inappropriate images.

Levi Richards, 1843

In this account Joseph mentions that the everlasting covenant has been broken.

David Nye White, 1843

Detailed that Joseph had been working the day before in a clearing and had left his axe in a stump and had returned there to pray. The two personages appearing at different times is also mentioned.

Alexander Neibaur, 1844

This account also details the personages appearing at separate times.

To read all the accounts go to:
www.churchofjesuschrist.org/study/manual/
gospel-topics-essays/first-vision-accounts

LUCY MACK SMITH'S NEAR DEATH EXPERIENCE

Joseph Smith Jr. was very much influenced by his mother Lucy Mac Smith's religious feelings and experience. We believe Lucy's near death experience had a significant impact on Joseph, because of its personal admonition to seek as well as the idea that God can answer a personal prayer.

Lucy's determination to keep her covenant seemed to manifest itself in her desire to bring her family into the Presbyterian faith. Joseph's response when he first returned from the vision is indicative of how much pressure he felt to join because he immediately tells her "I have learned for myself that Presbyterianism is not true." We have included Lucy's full account below for reference.

We had lived in Randolph but six months when I took a heavy cold, which caused a severe cough. To relieve this, every possible exertion was made, but it was all in vain. A hectic fever set in, which threatened to prove fatal, and the physician pronounced my case to be confirmed consumption.

During this sickness, my mother watched over me with much anxiety, sparing herself no pains in administering to my comfort, yet I continued to grow weaker and weaker, until I could scarcely endure even a foot-fall upon the floor, except in stocking-foot, and no one was allowed to speak in the room above a whisper.

While I was in this situation, a Methodist exhorter came to see me. On coming to the door, he knocked in his usual manner, and his knocking so agitated me that it was a considerable length of time before my nerves became altogether quieted again. My mother motioned him to a chair, and in a whisper informed him of my situation, which prevented his asking me any questions. He tarried some time, and while he sat he seemed deeply to meditate upon the uncertainty of my recovering; in the mean time, he showed a great desire to have conversation with me respecting my dying.

As he thus sat pondering, I fancied to myself that he was going to ask me if I was prepared to die, and I dreaded to have him speak to me, for then I did not consider myself ready for such an awful event, inasmuch as I knew not the ways of Christ; besides, there appeared to be a dark and lonesome chasm, between myself and the Savior, which I dared not attempt to pass.

I thought I strained my eyes, and by doing so I could discern a faint glimmer of the light that was beyond the gloom which lay immediately before me.

When I was meditating upon death, in this manner, my visitor left; soon after which my husband came to my bed, and took me by the hand, and said, "Oh, Lucy! my wife! my wife! you must die! The doctors have given you up; and all say you cannot live."

I then looked to the Lord, and begged and pleaded with him to spare my life, in order that I might bring up my children, and be a comfort to my husband. My mind was much agitated during the whole night. Sometimes I contemplated heaven and heavenly things; then my thoughts would turn upon those of earth — my babes and my companion.

During this night I made a solemn covenant with God, that, if he would let me live, I would endeavor to serve him according to the best of my abilities. Shortly after this, I heard a voice say to me, "Seek, and ye shall find; knock, and it shall be opened unto you. Let your heart be comforted; ye believe in God, believe also in me."

In a few moments my mother came in, and, looking upon me she said, "Lucy, you are better."

I replied, as my speech returned just at that instant, "Yes, mother, the Lord will let me live, if I am faithful to the promise which I made to him, to be a comfort to my mother, my husband, and my children." I continued to gain strength, until I became quite well as to my bodily health; but my mind was considerably disquieted. It was wholly occupied upon the subject of religion. As soon as I was able, I made all diligence in endeavoring to find some one who was capable of instructing me more perfectly in the way of life and salvation."

History of the Prophet Joseph Smith by His Mother Lucy Mack Smith, pg. 43-46

MAKING A PAGE OF PILLAR OF LIGHT

Creating each one of the pages of "Pillar of Light" takes a lot of time, patience and collaborative work. Here's how we did it.

STEP 1: THE SCRIPT

We start with a page of the script that Andrew wrote and researched using all four primary accounts, combined with the secondary accounts. The primary accounts were weighted as most important, and the secondary accounts as less important. The setting is described as well as suggestions on different shots or close-ups, similar to a movie script.

Page 1
Opening scene.
Close up of Joseph's face coming back into consciousness. Little spots of light can be seen around him.
[No text]
Cut to an establishing shot of Joseph lying on his back in a clearing in the Sacred Grove. A few stumps around him.
Joseph's narration (JN): "When I came to my senses, I found myself lying on my back."
Cut to Close up of Joseph's face showing a peaceful expression.
(JN) "My mind was in a state of calmness and peace indescribable."
Cut to Joseph slowly standing up and walking away
(JN) "I lay in wonder at what had been made known unto me and knew few would believe it."

STEP 2: ROUGHS & SCRIPT REVISIONS

Sal looks at the script and comes up with a rough idea of the page layout including number and size of panels, camera angles and placement of caption boxes and balloons. He experiments with different poses, facial expressions, compositions, and then sends his final rough to Andrew. Then, they discuss how the images are working to convey the story and what, if any, should be changed. This is also the point where decisions are made about adding additional text or if elements should be moved to the next page. Also costuming, or historical detail changes are discussed. For example, we decided to show a stump with his ax in it, and signs of clearing wood and chopping trees, so that was changed in the next step.

STEP 3: FINAL PENCILS & SCRIPT REVISIONS

Sal makes the changes that were discussed and then renders the final pencil drawing. This would also include making room for any new caption boxes that would be needed for additional text.

STEP 4: INKING & SCANNING

Sal draws over the final pencils with black ink, using tools like brushes, markers, crow-quill pens, etc. This is where he works out any additional shading and other fine details not included in the pencils. The finished page is then scanned at high resolution and "cleaned" in Photoshop.

STEP 5: FLAT COLORS

Andrew creates a flat color representation based on initial suggestions by Sal. These also serve as an efficient way to select areas for more detailed rendering or lighting effects that will happen in the next step.

STEP 6: COLORING–RENDERING & EFFECTS

After the flats are approved by Sal, Andrew works on rendering and lighting the page. Andrew then sends proofs to Sal who sends back changes with instructions and marks. Lighting effects will also be added. This will go back and forth until it is finished and approved by Sal.

STEP 7: LETTERING

After the colors are approved Andrew adds the lettering to the page. It sounds simple, but it can get very tricky trying to decide where to wrap words, which words to hyphenate, and where to place the caption boxes so they cover as little of the crucial art as possible. It's then sent to Sal who may suggest changes in positioning of the boxes for better flow of the eye. After those changes, it is finally done. Whew!!

ABOUT THE CREATORS

Andrew Knaupp & Sal Velluto

ANDREW KNAUPP is a visual artist and student of church history who has been passionate about telling the stories of the Prophet Joseph Smith and the Restoration from an early age. His interest increased after serving a mission in Ohio, where he was able to view many early church history sites.

He helped create *The Book of Mormon on Trial,* and *The Golden Plates* graphic novels, as well as creating a series of paintings about Joseph Smith's imprisonments called Prisons and Prophets. He has a BFA from Brigham Young University in Illustration.

Andrew Knaupp lives in Lindon Utah with his wife Stefani and their three children.

SAL VELLUTO's professional career in comics started in 1986. Since then, the Italian born - Utah resident has been working for major American publishers (Marvel, DC, Valiant) several independents as well as international publishers from Italy, Sweden, and Australia.

From 1991 to 2002 Sal drew *Black Panther* for Marvel Comics, thus becoming the most prolific artist, to date, on this title. Some of Sal's original design ideas for *Black Panther* were used in the 2019 Oscar-winning movie.

Sal Velluto and his wife of 34 years, Sharon, live in West Jordan, Utah. They have four children and one grandchild.

ACKNOWLEDGEMENTS
We want to thank the following generous donors whose contributions made this project possible.

Carol Beck, Jan Eversole, Danny & Jason Kilgore, Tony Hoffmann, Tom Holdman, Beci Baguley, Theric Jepson, Rachel Thacker, Lara Dean, Edmond Ashworth, Joe & Ann Dupaix, Bob Bedore, Jonathan Olson, Todd Tritsch, Chris Gillis, Martha Clanton, Michael Booth, Connor Rawle, Kim Scott, Kitty Harmon, Chris Calkins, Carol E, Chester Cox, Michelle McKinley, Kristina Crockett, Thomas Harmon, Michael Zurligen, Valerie Knaupp, Sean Hanna, Nicole Taggart, Mike Lovins, Bob Pollnow, Joanne Kapp, Don Shillcox, Trevor Alvord, Tamlyn Laurence, Sean Vassilaros, Mark Berends, Jennifer Nelson, Kristin McMurray, Linda Hyde, Wes Mashburn, Kimberly Dawson, Carol Kwant, Elisabeth Holley, Amanda Maldonado, Kathy & Dave, Joseph Kendrick, Kay Henningson, Gilbert Warner, Fray T, Larry Hanson, Jeana Rock, Kris Kearns, Lorraine Wilson, Claire Johnson, and many others.